Quick and Easy Air Fryer Recipes Cookbook

Quick, Healthy, Easy And Delicious Recipes For the whole family

Written By

Marion Bartolini

Table of Contents

INTRODUCTION 9

BREAKFAST RECIPES 11

   Kale potato nuggets.. 12

   Air fried falafel 14

   Veggie bites 16

   Fried mushrooms... 18

   General Tso's cauliflower 20

BRUNCH RECIPES 23

   Spinach frittata 24

LUNCH RECIPES.. 27

   Cheeseburger egg rolls 28

   Crispy Mongolian beef... 30

   Copycat taco bell crunch wraps... 32

   Beef taco fried egg rolls 33

   Pub style corned beef egg rolls 35

   Reuben egg rolls 37

   Beef empanadas 38

   Lamb fritters 39

   Lasagna casserole 40

   Beef and chorizo burger 42

   Filet mignon with chili peanut sauce 43

   Irish whisky steak.. 44

   Hungarian beef goulash... 45

   Saucy beef with cotija cheese 47

DINNER RECIPES 49

   Mussels bowls... 50

Fall-off-the-bone chicken 51

White chicken chili 52

SIDE DISH RECIPES 53

Colby Potato Patties 54

Turkey Garlic Potatoes 56

CASSEROLES 57

Cheesy sausage and broccoli casserole 58

CHICKEN AND POULTRY 61

Tandoori chicken 62

Baked Thai peanut chicken egg rolls 64

Chick fila chicken sandwich 66

Chicken fried rice 68

BEEF, STEAK AND LAMB RECIPES 71

Crumbed rack of lamb 72

Sweet and Sour Delicious Pork 74

FISH AND SEAFOODS 77

Fried Crawfish 78

Prawn Burgers 79

Jumbo Shrimp 80

FRUIT AND VEGETABLES 81

Mini zucchini's and feta 82

SNACK RECIPES 85

Fried pickles 86

Crusted mozzarella sticks 88

Sesame nuggets 89

Fried parmesan zucchini 91

Radish chips 93

APPETIZER RECIPES 95

Cremini mushroom satay 96

PASTA AND RICE RECIPES 97

Lemony Parmesan Risotto with Peas 98

BREAD & GRAINS 101

Baguette bread 102

DESSERT RECIPES 105

Red Wine Muffins 106

Tea Cupcake 107

Rustic Cheesecake 109

Lemon Cake with Cheese Meringue 111

Creamy Sponge Cake 113

Banana Inverted Cake 114

Yogurt Cake 116

CONCLUSION 117

INTRODUCTION

Thank you for purchasing this book!

Healthy foods

The air fryer is quite popular, owing to producing healthy meals. It reduces oils and fats, thereby making the result relatively healthy. The same cannot be said about standard cooking techniques where you must add in lots of oils and fats. These can adversely affect your health and be the reason for obesity and illnesses. Therefore, an air fryer is best suited for improving their health by making changes in their cooking habits.

Enjoy your reading!

BREAKFAST RECIPES

Kale potato nuggets

Preparation time: 15 minutes

Cooking time: 18 minutes

Serving: 4

Ingredients:

- 2 cups potatoes, chopped
- 1 teaspoon olive oil
- 1 garlic clove, minced
- 4 cups kale, chopped
- 1/8 cup almond milk
- 1/4 teaspoon sea salt
- 1/8 teaspoon ground black pepper
- Vegetable oil spray as needed

Directions:

1. Set a cooking pot filled with water over medium heat.
2. Add potatoes to this boiling water and cook for 30 minutes until soft.

3. Meanwhile, sauté garlic with oil in a skillet over medium high heat until golden.

4. Stir in kale and sauté for 3 minutes., then transfer this mixture to a bowl.

5. Drain the boiled potatoes and add them to the kale.

6. Mix the potatoes with a potato masher.

7. Stir in salt, black pepper, and milk them, mix well.

8. Make 1inch potato nuggets out of this mixture.

9. Place these nuggets in the air fryer basket.

10. Return the air fryer basket to the air fryer.

11. Select the air fry mode at 390° f for 15 minutes.

12. Flip the nuggets once cooked halfway through, then resume cooking. Serve warm.

Nutrition: Calories 113 Fat 3g Carbs 20g Fiber 3g Sugar 1g Protein 5g

Air fried falafel

Preparation time: 15 minutes

Cooking time: 10 minutes

Serving: 6

Ingredients:

- 1 1/2 cups dry garbanzo beans
- 1/2 cup fresh parsley, chopped
- 1/2 cup fresh cilantro, chopped
- 1/2 cup white onion, chopped
- 7 garlic cloves, minced
- 2 tablespoons all-purpose flour
- 1/2 teaspoons sea salt
- 1 tablespoon ground cumin
- 1/8 teaspoons ground cardamom
- 1 teaspoon ground coriander
- 1/8 teaspoons cayenne pepper

Directions:

1. Soak garbanzo beans in a bowl filled with water for 24 hours.
2. Drain and transfer the beans to a cooking pot filled with water.
3. Cook the beans for 1 hour or more on simmer until soft.
4. Add cilantro, onion, garlic, and parsley to a food processor and blend until finely chopped.
5. Drain the cooked garbanzo beans and transfer them to the food processor.
6. Add salt, cardamom, cayenne, coriander, cumin, and flour.
7. Blend until it makes a rough dough.
8. Transfer this falafel mixture to a bowl, cover with a plastic wrap and refrigerate for 2 hours.
9. Make 1 ½ inches balls out of this bean's mixture.
10. Lightly press the balls and place them in the air fryer basket.
11. Return the air fryer basket to the air fryer.
12. Select the air fry mode at 400° f for 10 minutes.
13. Flip the falafels once cooked halfway through the resume cooking.
14. Serve warm.

Nutrition: Calories 206; Fat 4g; Carbs 35g; Fiber 4g; Sugar 9g; Protein 16g

Veggie bites

Preparation time: 10 minutes

Cooking time: 45 minutes

Serving: 6

Ingredients:

- 1 large broccoli, cut into florets
- 6 large carrots, diced
- A handful of garden peas
- 1/2 cauliflower, riced
- 1 large onion, peeled and diced
- 1 small zucchini, diced
- 2 leeks, sliced
- 1 can coconut milk
- 2 oz. Plain flour
- 1 cm cube ginger peeled and grated
- 1 tablespoon garlic puree
- 1 tablespoon olive oil
- 1 tablespoon Thai green curry paste

16

- 1 tablespoon coriander
- 1 tablespoon mixed spice
- 1 teaspoon cumin
- Salt and black pepper, to taste

Directions:

1. Place leek and courgette in a steamer basket and steam them for 20 minutes.
2. Sauté onion, ginger, and garlic with olive oil in a skillet until soft.
3. Add steamed leek and courgette to the skillet and sauté for 5 minutes.
4. Stir in coconut milk and the rest of the spices.
5. Mix well, then add the cauliflower rice then cook for 10 minutes.
6. Remove the hot skillet from the heat and allow it to cool.
7. Cover and refrigerate this mixture for 1 hour.
8. Slice the mixture into bite size pieces and place these pieces in the air fryer basket.
9. Return the air fryer basket to the air fryer.
10. Select the air fry mode at 350 degrees f for 10 minutes.
11. Carefully flip the bites once cooked halfway through, then resume cooking. Serve warm.

Nutrition: Calories 270; Fat 16g; Carbs 33g; Fiber 5g; Sugar 7g; Protein 4g

Fried mushrooms

Preparation time: 15 minutes

Cooking time: 25 minutes

Serving: 6

Ingredients:

- 2 cups oyster mushrooms
- 1 cup buttermilk
- 1 ½ cups all-purpose flour
- 1 teaspoon salt
- 1 teaspoon black pepper
- 1 teaspoon garlic powder
- 1 teaspoon onion powder
- 1 teaspoon smoked paprika
- 1 teaspoon cumin
- 1 tablespoon oil

Directions:

1. At 375 degrees f, preheat your air fryer on air fry mode.

2. Clean the mushrooms and then soak them in buttermilk for 15 minutes.

3. Mix all-purpose flour with onion powder, garlic powder, black pepper, salt, smoked paprika, and cumin in a suitable bowl.

4. Coat the mushrooms with flour mixture and then dip again with buttermilk.

5. Coat the mushrooms again with flour and buttermilk.

6. Place the coated mushrooms in the air fryer basket.

7. Return the air fryer basket to the air fryer and cook for 10 minutes.

8. Flip the mushrooms once cooked halfway through. Serve warm.

Nutrition: Calories 166; Fat 2g; Carbs 28g; Fiber 8g; Sugar 7g; Protein 8g

General Tso's cauliflower

Preparation time: 15 minutes

Cooking time: 28 minutes

Serving:4

Ingredients:

- Cauliflower
- 1/2 head cauliflower, cut into florets
- 1/2 cup flour
- 2 large eggs, whisked
- 1 cup panko breadcrumbs
- 1/4 teaspoons salt
- 1/4 teaspoons black pepper
- General Tso's sauce
- 1 tablespoon sesame oil
- 2 garlic cloves, minced
- 1 tablespoon fresh ginger, grated
- 1/2 cup vegetable broth

- 1/4 cup of soy sauce
- 1/4 cup of rice vinegar
- 1/4 cup brown sugar
- 2 tablespoons tomato paste
- 2 tablespoons cornstarch
- 2 tablespoons cold water

Directions:

1. At 400 degrees f, preheat your ninja air fryer on air fry mode.
2. Whisk egg in one bowl spread panko in another bowl and add flour to another bowl.
3. Dredge the cauliflower through the flour, dip in the egg and then coat with breadcrumbs.
4. Place the prepared cauliflower florets in the air fryer basket.
5. Return the air fryer basket to the air fryer and cook for 20 minutes.
6. Flip the florets once cooked halfway through, then resume cooking.
7. Meanwhile, sauté ginger, garlic, and sesame oil in a saucepan for 2 minutes.
8. Stir in the rest of the sauce ingredients except cornstarch.
9. Mix cornstarch with 2 tablespoons water in a bowl.
10. Pour the slurry into the sauce, mix, and cook until the sauce thickens.
11. Get the sauce from the heat and allow it to cool.
12. Toss in the baked cauliflower and mix well to coat. Serve warm.

Nutrition: Calories 288; Fat 9g; Sodium 761mg; Carbs 46g; Fiber 4g; Sugar 12g; Protein 6g

BRUNCH RECIPES

Spinach frittata

Preparation time: 5 minutes

Cooking time: 8 minutes

Servings: 1

Ingredients:

- 3 eggs
- 1 cup spinach, chopped
- 1 small onion, minced
- 2 tbsp mozzarella cheese, grated
- Pepper
- Salt

Directions:

1. Preheat the air fryer to 350° f.
2. Spray air fryer pan with cooking spray.
3. In a bowl, whisk eggs with remaining ingredients until well combined.

4. Pour egg mixture into the prepared pan and place pan in the air fryer basket.

5. Cook frittata for 8 minutes or until set.

6. Serve and enjoy.

Nutrition: Calories 384 Fat 23 g Carbohydrates 17 g Sugar 1 g Protein 33 g

LUNCH RECIPES

Cheeseburger egg rolls

Preparation time: 15 minutes

Cooking Time: 10 minutes

Servings: 6

Ingredients:

- 6 egg roll wrappers
- 6 chopped dill pickle chips
- 1 tbsp. Yellow mustard
- 3 tbsp. Cream cheese
- 3 tbsp. Shredded cheddar cheese
- ½ c. Chopped onion
- ½ c. Chopped bell pepper
- ¼ tsp. Onion powder
- ¼ tsp. Garlic powder
- 8 ounces of raw lean ground beef

Directions:

1. In a skillet, add seasonings, beef, onion, and bell pepper. Stir and crumble beef till fully cooked, and vegetables are soft.
2. Take skillet off the heat and add cream cheese, mustard, and cheddar cheese, stirring till melted.
3. Pour beef mixture into a bowl and fold in pickles.

4. Lay out egg wrappers and place 1/6th of beef mixture into each one. Moisten egg roll wrapper edges with water. Fold sides to the middle and seal with water.
5. Repeat with all other egg rolls.
6. Place rolls into air fryer, one batch at a time. Cook 7-9 minutes at 392 °F.

Nutrition: Calories: 153 Fat: 4g Protein: 12g Sugar: 3g

Crispy Mongolian beef

Preparation time: 10 minutes

Cooking time: 12 minutes

Servings: 6-10

Ingredients:

- Olive oil
- ½ c. Almond flour
- 2 pounds beef tenderloin or beef chuck, sliced into strips

Sauce:

- ½ c. Chopped green onion
- 1 tsp. Red chili flakes
- 1 tsp. Almond flour
- ½ c. Brown sugar
- 1 tsp. Hoisin sauce
- ½ c. Water
- ½ c. Rice vinegar
- ½ c. Low-sodium soy sauce
- 1 tbsp. Chopped garlic
- 1 tbsp. Finely chopped ginger
- 2 tbsp. Olive oil

Directions:

1. Toss strips of beef in almond flour, ensuring they are coated well.
2. Add to air fryer and cook 10 minutes at 300 °F.

3. Meanwhile, add all sauce ingredients to the pan and bring to a boil. Mix well.

4. Add beef strips to the sauce and cook 2 minutes.

5. Serve over cauliflower rice!

Nutrition: Calories: 290 Fat: 14g Protein: 22g Sugar: 1g

Copycat taco bell crunch wraps

Preparation time: 5 minutes

Cooking time: 5 minutes

Servings: 6

Ingredients:

- 6 wheat tostadas
- 2 c. Sour cream
- 2 c. Mexican blend cheese
- 2 c. Shredded lettuce
- 12 ounces low-sodium nacho cheese
- 3 roman tomatoes
- 6 12-inch wheat tortillas
- 1 1/3 c. Water
- 2 packets low-sodium taco seasoning
- 2 pounds of lean ground beef

Directions:

1. Ensure your air fryer is preheated to 400 °F.
2. Make beef according to taco seasoning packets.
3. Place 2/3 c. Prepared beef, 4 tbsp. Cheese, 1 tostada, 1/3 c. Sour cream, 1/3 c. Lettuce, 1/6th of tomatoes and 1/3 c. Cheese on each tortilla.
4. Fold up tortillas edges and repeat with remaining ingredients.
5. Lay the folded sides of tortillas down into the air fryer and spray with olive oil.
6. Cook 2 minutes till browned.

Nutrition: Calories: 311 Fat: 9g Protein: 22g Sugar: 2g

Beef taco fried egg rolls

Preparation Time: 15 minutes

Cooking Time: 10 minutes

Servings: 8

Ingredients:

- 1 tsp. cilantro
- 2 chopped garlic cloves
- 1 tbsp. olive oil
- 1 C. shredded Mexican cheese
- ½ packet taco seasoning
- ½ can cilantro lime
- ½ chopped onion
- egg roll wrappers
- 1-pound lean ground beef

Directions:

1. Ensure that the air fryer is turn on to 400 °F.
2. Add onions and garlic to a skillet, cooking till fragrant. Then add taco seasoning, pepper, salt, and beef, cooking till beef is broke up into tiny pieces and cooked thoroughly.
3. Add cilantro and stir well.
4. Lay out egg wrappers and brush with water to soften a bit.
5. Load wrappers with beef filling and add cheese to each.

33

6. Fold diagonally to close and use water to secure edges.

7. Brush filled egg wrappers with olive oil and add to the air fryer.

8. Cook 8 minutes, flip, and cook another 4 minutes.

9. Served sprinkled with cilantro.

Nutrition: Calories: 348 Fat: 11g Protein: 24g Sugar: 1g

Pub style corned beef egg rolls

Preparation time: 5 minutes

Cooking time: 15 minutes

Servings: 10

Ingredients:

- Olive oil
- ½ c. Orange marmalade
- 5 slices of swiss cheese
- 4 c. Corned beef and cabbage
- 1 egg
- 10 egg roll wrappers
- Brandy mustard sauce:
- 1/16th tsp. Pepper
- 2 tbsp. Whole grain mustard
- 1 tsp. Dry mustard powder
- 1 c. Heavy cream
- ½ c. Chicken stock
- ¼ c. Brandy
- ¾ c. Dry white wine
- ¼ tsp. Curry powder
- ½ tbsp. Cilantro
- 1 minced shallot
- 2 tbsp. Ghee

Directions:

1. To make mustard sauce, add shallots and ghee to skillet, cooking until softened. Then add brandy and wine, heating to a low boil. Cook 5 minutes for liquids to reduce. Add stock and seasonings. Simmer 5 minutes.

2. Turn down heat and add heavy cream. Cook on low till sauce reduces and it covers the back of a spoon.

3. Place sauce in the fridge to chill.

4. Crack the egg in a bowl and set to the side.

5. Lay out an egg wrapper with the corner towards you. Brush the edges with egg wash.

6. Place 1/3 cup of corned beef mixture into the center along with 2 tablespoons of marmalade and ½ a slice of swiss cheese.

7. Fold the bottom corner over filling. As you are folding the sides, make sure they are stick well to the first flap you made.

8. Place filled rolls into prepared air fryer basket. Spritz rolls with olive oil.

9. Cook 10 minutes at 390 °F, shaking halfway through cooking.

10. Serve rolls with brandy mustard sauce and devour!

Nutrition: Calories: 415 Fat: 13g Protein: 38g Sugar: 4g

Reuben egg rolls

Preparation time: 5 minutes

Cooking time: 15 minutes

Servings: 10

Ingredients:

- Swiss cheese
- Can of sauerkraut
- Sliced deli corned beef
- Egg roll wrappers

Directions:

1. Cut corned beef and swiss cheese into thin slices.
2. Drain sauerkraut and dry well.
3. Take egg roll wrapper and moisten edges with water.
4. Stack center with corned beef and cheese till you reach desired thickness. Top off with sauerkraut.
5. Fold corner closest to you over the edge of filling. Bring up sides and glue with water.
6. Add to air fryer basket and spritz with olive oil.
7. Cook 4 minutes at 400 °F, then flip and cook another 4 minutes.

Nutrition: Calories: 251 Fat: 12g Protein: 31g Sugar: 4g

Beef empanadas

Preparation time: 15 minutes

Cooking time: 15 minutes

Servings: 8

Ingredients:

- 1 tsp. water
- 1 egg white
- 1 C. picadillo
- Goya empanada discs (thawed)

Directions:

1. Ensure your air fryer is preheated to 325. Spray basket with olive oil.
2. Place 2 tablespoons of picadillo into the center of each disc. Fold disc in half and use a fork to seal edges. Repeat with all ingredients.
3. Whisk egg white with water and brush tops of empanadas with egg wash.
4. Add 2-3 empanadas to air fryer, cooking 8 minutes until golden. Repeat till you cook all filled empanadas.

Nutrition: Calories: 183 Fat: 5g Protein: 11g Sugar: 2g

Lamb fritters

Preparation time: 10 minutes

Cooking time: 30 minutes

Servings: 8

Ingredients:

- 2 ½ lb. lamb meat, ground
- 2 spring onions; chopped
- ½ cup almond meal
- eggs, whisked
- 1 tbsp. garlic; minced
- 2 tbsp. cilantro; chopped
- Zest of 1 lemon
- Juice of 1 lemon
- Cooking spray
- 2 tbsp. mint; chopped
- A pinch of salt and black pepper

Directions:

1. Take bowl and mix all the ingredients except the cooking spray, stir well and shape medium cakes out of this mix
2. Put the cakes in your air fryer, grease them with cooking spray and cook at 390°F for 15 minutes on each side
3. Split between plates and serve with side salad

Nutrition: Calories: 283; Fat: 13g; Fiber: 4g; Carbs: 6g; Protein: 15g

Lasagna casserole

Preparation time: 15 minutes

Cooking time: 15 minutes

Servings: 4

Ingredients:

- ¾ cup low-carb no-sugar-added pasta sauce
- 1 lb. 80/20 ground beef; cooked and drained
- ½ cup full-fat ricotta cheese
- ¼ cup grated parmesan cheese.
- ½ tsp. Garlic powder.
- 1 tsp. Dried parsley.
- ½ tsp. Dried oregano.
- 1 cup shredded mozzarella cheese

Directions:

1. In a 4-cup round baking dish, pour ¼ cup pasta sauce on the bottom of the dish. Place ¼ of the ground beef on top of the sauce.
2. In a small bowl, mix ricotta, parmesan, garlic powder, parsley and oregano. Place dollops of half the mixture on top of the beef
3. Sprinkle with ⅓ of the mozzarella. Repeat layers until all beef, ricotta mixture, sauce and mozzarella are used, ending with the mozzarella on top

4. Cover dish with foil and place into the air fryer basket. Adjust the temperature to 370 °F and set the timer for 15 minutes. In the last 2 minutes of cooking, remove the foil to brown the cheese. Serve immediately.

Nutrition: Calories: 371; Protein: 34g; Fiber: 6g; Fat: 24g; Carbs: 8g

Beef and chorizo burger

Preparation Time: 10 minutes

Cooking Time: 15 minutes

Servings: 4

Ingredients:

- 5 slices pickled jalapeños; chopped
- ¼ lb. Mexican-style ground chorizo
- ¾lb. 80/20 ground beef.
- ¼ cup chopped onion
- ¼ tsp. Cumin
- 1 tsp. Minced garlic
- 2 tsp. Chili powder

Directions:

1. Take a large bowl, mix all ingredients. Divide the mixture into four sections and form them into burger patties.
2. Place burger patties into the air fryer basket, working in batches if necessary. Adjust the temperature to 375 °F and set the timer for 15 minutes
3. Flip the patties halfway through the cooking time. Serve warm.

Nutrition: Calories: 291; Protein: 26g; Fiber: 9g; Fat: 13g; Carbs: 7g

Filet mignon with chili peanut sauce

Preparation Time: 2 hours

Cooking Time: 20 minutes

Servings: 4

Ingredients

- 2 pounds filet mignon, sliced into bite-sized strips
- 1 tablespoon oyster sauce
- 2 tablespoons sesame oil
- 2 tablespoons tamari sauce
- 1 tablespoon ginger-garlic paste
- 1 tablespoon mustard
- 1 teaspoon chili powder
- 1/4 cup peanut butter
- 2 tablespoons lime juice
- 1 teaspoon red pepper flakes
- 2 tablespoons water

Directions

1. Place the beef strips, oyster sauce, sesame oil, tamari sauce, ginger-garlic paste, mustard, and chili powder in a large ceramic dish.
2. Cover and allow it to marinate for 2 hours in your refrigerator.
3. Cook in the preheated air fryer at 400 °F for 18 minutes, shaking the basket occasionally.
4. Mix the peanut butter with lime juice, red pepper flakes, and water. Spoon the sauce onto the air fried beef strips and serve warm.

Nutrition: 420 Calories; 21g Fat; 5g Carbs; 50g Protein; 7g Sugars; 1g Fiber

Irish whisky steak

Ingredients Preparation Time: 2 hours

Cooking Time: 22 minutes

Servings: 6

Ingredients

- 2 pounds sirloin steaks
- 1 ½tablespoons tamari sauce
- 1/3 teaspoon cayenne pepper
- 1/3 teaspoon ground ginger
- 2 garlic cloves, thinly sliced
- 2 tablespoons Irish whiskey
- 2 tablespoons olive oil
- Fine sea salt, to taste

Directions

1. Firstly, add all the ingredients, minus the olive oil and the steak, to a resealable plastic bag.
2. Throw in the steak and let it marinate for a couple of hours. After that, drizzle the sirloin steaks with 2 tablespoons olive oil.
3. Roast for approximately 22 minutes at 395 °F, turning it halfway through the time. Bon appétit!

Nutrition: 260 Calories; 17g Fat; 8g Carbs; 35g Protein; 2g Sugars; 1g Fiber

Hungarian beef goulash

Preparation Time: 10 minutes

Cooking Time: 1 hour

Servings: 4

Ingredients

- Sea salt and cracked black pepper, to taste
- 1 teaspoon Hungarian paprika
- 1 ½ pounds beef chuck roast, boneless, cut into bite-sized cubes
- 2 teaspoons sunflower oil
- 1 medium-sized leek, chopped
- 2 garlic cloves, minced
- 2 bay leaves
- 1 teaspoon caraway seeds.
- 2 cups roasted vegetable broth
- 1 ripe tomato, pureed
- 2 tablespoons red wine
- 2 bell peppers, chopped
- 1 celery stalk, peeled and diced

Directions

1. Add the salt, black pepper, Hungarian paprika, and beef to a resealable bag; shake to coat well.
2. Heat the oil in a Dutch oven over medium-high flame; sauté the leeks, garlic, bay leaves, and caraway seeds about 4 minutes or until fragrant. Transfer to a lightly greased baking pan.

3. Then, brown the beef, stirring occasionally, working in batches. Add to the baking pan.

4. Add the vegetable broth, tomato, and red wine. Lower the pan onto the air fryer basket. Bake at 325 °F for 40 minutes.

5. Add the bell peppers and celery. Cook an additional 20 minutes. Serve immediately and enjoy!

Nutrition: 306 Calories; 11g Fat; 8g Carbs; 36g Protein; 6g Sugars; 8g Fiber

Saucy beef with cotija cheese

Preparation Time: 5 minutes

Cooking Time: 22 minutes

Servings: 3

Ingredients

- 2 ounces cotija cheese, cut into sticks
- 2 teaspoons paprika
- 2 teaspoons dried thyme
- 1/2 cup shallots, peeled and chopped
- 3 beef tenderloins, cut in half lengthwise
- 2 teaspoons dried basil
- 1/3 cup homemade bone stock
- 2 tablespoon olive oil
- 3 cloves garlic, minced
- 1 ½ cups tomato puree, no sugar added
- 1 teaspoon ground black pepper, or more to taste
- 1 teaspoon fine sea salt, or more to taste

Directions

1. Firstly, season the beef tenderloin with the salt, ground black pepper, and paprika; place a piece of the cotija cheese in the middle.
2. Now, tie each tenderloin with a kitchen string; drizzle with olive oil and reserve.

3. Stir the garlic, shallots, bone stock, tomato puree into an oven safe bowl; cook in the preheated air fryer at 375 °F for 7 minutes.

4. Add the reserved beef along with basil and thyme. Set the timer for 14 minutes. Eat warm and enjoy!

Nutrition: 589 Calories; 47g Fat; 3g Carbs; 31g Protein; 5g Sugars; 2g Fiber

DINNER RECIPES

Mussels bowls

Preparation time: 5 minutes

Cooking time: 12 minutes

Servings: 2

Ingredients:

- 2 pounds mussels, scrubbed
- 12 ounces black beer
- 1 tablespoon olive oil
- 1 yellow onion, chopped
- 8 ounces spicy sausage, chopped
- 1 tablespoon paprika

Directions:

1. Combine all the ingredients in a pan that fits your air fryer.
2. Place the pan in the air fryer and cook at 400 °F for 12 minutes.
3. Divide the mussels into bowls, serve, and enjoy!

Nutrition: calories 201 fat 6 fiber 7 carbs 17 protein 7

Fall-off-the-bone chicken

Preparation time: 10 minutes

Cooking time: 1hour and 10 minutes

Servings: 4

Ingredients:

- 1 tbsp. Packed brown sugar
- 1 tbsp. Chili powder
- 1 tbsp. Smoked paprika
- 1 tsp. Chopped thyme leaves
- ¼ tbsp. Kosher salt
- ¼ tbsp. Black pepper
- 1 whole small chicken
- 1 tbsp. Extra-virgin olive oil
- 2/3 c. Low-sodium chicken broth
- 2 tbsp. Chopped parsley

Directions:

1. Coat chicken with brown sugar, chili powder, sugar, pepper, paprika, and thyme.
2. Sauté chicken in oil for 3-4 minutes
3. Pour broth in the pot.
4. Pressure cook on high for 25 minutes
5. Garnish sliced chicken with parsley and serve.

Nutrition: calories 1212 fat 10g carbs 31g protein 15g

White chicken chili

Preparation time: 5 minutes

Cooking time: 30 minutes

Servings: 6

Ingredients:

- 1 tbsp. Vegetable oil
- 1 red bell pepper, diced
- .15 oz. Condensed cream of chicken soup
- 5 tbsp. Shredded cheddar cheese
- 2 green onions, sliced
- 1 cup kernel corn
- 1 tbsp. Chili powder
- 6 oz. (2boneless, skinless chicken breast)
- 15 oz. White cannellini beans
- 1 cup chunky salsa

Directions:

1. Sauté pepper, corn, and chili powder in oil for 2 minutes
2. Season chicken with salt and pepper.
3. Layer the beans, salsa, water, chicken, and soup over the corn mixture.
4. Pressure cook on high for 4 minutes
5. Shred chicken and return to pot.
6. Serve topped with cheese and green onions.

Nutrition: calories 1848 fat 70g carbs 204g protein 90g

SIDE DISH RECIPES

Colby Potato Patties

Preparation Time: 5 minutes

Cooking Time: 15 minutes

Servings: 8

Ingredients

- 2 lb. white potatoes, peeled and grated
- ½ cup scallions, finely chopped
- ½ tsp. freshly ground black pepper
- 1tbsp. fine sea salt
- ½ tsp. hot paprika
- 2 cups Colby cheese, shredded
- ¼ cup canola oil
- 1 cup crushed crackers

Directions:

1. Boil the potatoes until soft. Dry them off and peel them before mashing thoroughly, leaving no lumps.
2. Combine the mashed potatoes with scallions, pepper, salt, paprika, and cheese.
3. Shape mixture into balls with your hands and press with your palm to flatten them into patties.
4. In shallow dish, combine the canola oil and crushed crackers. Coat the patties in the crumb mixture.

5. Cook the patties at 360°F for about 10 minutes, in multiple batches if necessary.

6. Serve with tabasco mayo or the sauce of your choice.

Nutrition: Calories: 130 Fat: 7g Carbs: 17g Protein: 1g

Turkey Garlic Potatoes

Preparation Time: 10 minutes

Cooking Time: 45 minutes

Servings: 2

Ingredients

- unsmoked turkey strips
- small potatoes
- 1 tsp. garlic, minced
- 2 tsp. olive oil
- Salt to taste
- Pepper to taste

Directions:

1. Peel the potatoes and cube them finely.
2. Coat in 1 teaspoon of oil and cook in the Air Fryer for 10 minutes at 350°F.
3. In separate bowl, slice the turkey finely and combine with the garlic, oil, salt and pepper. Pour the potatoes into the bowl and mix well.
4. Lay the mixture on some silver aluminum foil, transfer to the fryer and cook for about 10 minutes.
5. Serve with raita.

Nutrition: Calories: 210 Fat: 4g Carbs: 22g Protein: 22g

CASSEROLES

Cheesy sausage and broccoli casserole

Preparation time: 10 minutes

Cooking time: 20 minutes

Servings: 8

Ingredients:

- 10 eggs
- 1 cup cheddar cheese, shredded and divided
- ¾ cup heavy whipping cream
- 1 (12ounce / 340g package cooked chicken sausage
- 1 cup broccoli, chopped
- 2 cloves garlic, minced
- ½ tablespoon salt
- ¼ tablespoon ground black pepper
- Cooking spray

Directions:

1. Spritz a baking pan with cooking spray.
2. Whisk the eggs with cheddar and cream in a large bowl to mix well.

3. Combine the cooked sausage, broccoli, salt, garlic, and ground black pepper in a separate bowl. Stir to mix well.

4. Put sausage mixture into the baking pan, then spread the egg mixture over to cover.

5. Put the baking pan in the air fryer. Cook at the corresponding preset mode or air fry at 400°F (204°C until the eggs are set).

6. Serve immediately.

Nutrition: Calories: 370 Fat: 20g Carbs: 32g Protein: 17g

CHICKEN AND POULTRY

Tandoori chicken

Preparation time: 30 minutes

Cooking time: 15 minutes

Servings: 2

Ingredients:

For the tandoori chicken:

- 1/2 chicken, halved
- 2 cloves garlic, peeled, minced
- 1/2 tbsp fresh ginger, minced
- 1/4 cup yogurt (Greek)
- 1/2 tsp chili powder
- 1/2 tsp salt or to taste
- 1/2 tsp turmeric powder

- Drops of orange food coloring
- 1/2 tsp garam masala
- Cooking spray or oil for basting

To serve (optional:

- Lemon wedges to serve
- A handful fresh cilantro, chopped, to garnish
- Sliced onions to serve

Directions:

1. Add garlic, chili, ginger, powder, salt, food coloring, turmeric powder, yogurt, and garam masala into a bowl and mix well.
2. Marinate the chicken with this mixture. Refrigerate for about 30 minutes.
3. Place the chicken pieces (without the marinade in the air fryer basket).
4. Spray a little cooking spray or brush with oil. Flip sides and spray again with cooking spray.
5. Air fry in a preheated fryer at 400 °F for 12 minutes. Flip sides after 6 minutes of cooking, spraying some more oil over the chicken.
6. Air fry until the internal temperature of the meat shows 165 °F on a meat cooking thermometer.
7. Serve with sliced onions and lemon wedges.

Nutrition: Calories: 178 Fat: 6 g Carb: 2 g Protein: 25 g

Baked Thai peanut chicken egg rolls

Preparation time: 10 minutes

Cooking time: 8 minutes

Servings: 2

Ingredients:

- 2 egg roll wrappers
- 2 tbsps. Thai peanut sauce
- 2 green onions, chopped
- 1/2 cup shredded rotisserie chicken
- 1 small carrot, very thinly sliced
- 1/8 red peppers, sliced

Directions:

1. Place chicken in a bowl. Spread Thai peanut sauce over the chicken.
2. Place the egg roll wrappers on your countertop. Divide equally—carrot, onion, and bell pepper—and place on the wrappers' bottom third. Divide the chicken and place over the vegetables.

64

3. Brush the edges of the wrappers with water. Fold the sides slightly over the filling and then roll the wrappers tightly. Cover with moist paper towels until ready to fry.

4. Spray the egg rolls all over with cooking spray. Place in the air fryer basket.

5. Air fry in a preheated fryer at 390 °F for 6–8 minutes or until crisp.

6. Chop into 2 halves and serve with Thai peanut sauce.

Nutrition: Calories: 235 Fat: 2 g Carb: 17 g Protein: 21 g

Chick fila chicken sandwich

Preparation time: 10 minutes

Cooking time: 14 minutes

Servings: 3

Ingredients:

- 1 chicken breast, skinless, boneless, half an inch in thickness
- 1 egg
- 1/2 cup flour (all-purpose)
- 1 tbsp potato starch
- 1/2 tsp sea salt
- 1/4 tsp garlic powder
- 1/2 tbsp extra virgin olive oil
- 2–3 hamburger buns, toasted, buttered
- 1/4 cup dill pickle juice
- 1/4 cup milk
- 1 tbsp powdered sugar
- 1/2 tsp paprika
- Ground pepper as per taste

- ⅛ tsp ground celery seeds
- Dill pickle chips to serve
- Cayenne pepper as per taste (optional
- Mayonnaise to serve

Directions:

1. Chop chicken into 2–3 parts.
2. Add chicken and pickle juice into a Ziplock bag and seal it. Turn the bag a few times so that the chicken is well coated with the pickle juice. Chill for 30–60 minutes.
3. Add egg and milk to a bowl and whisk well.
4. Add flour, potato starch, and all the spices in another shallow bowl.
5. First, dip chicken in the egg mixture. Shake to drop off excess egg.
6. Next, dredge in the flour mixture. Shake to drop off excess flour. This step is necessary.
7. Put oil in the air fryer basket. Add the chicken pieces to the air fryer basket. Spray some cooking spray over the chicken.
8. Air fry in a preheated air fryer at 340 °F for 12 minutes. Flip sides after 6 minutes of cooking, spraying some more oil over the chicken.
9. Increase the temperature to 400 °F. Cook for 2 minutes. Turn to sides and cook the other side for 2 minutes.
10. 1place the chicken on the bottom half of the burger buns. Drop some mayonnaise over it. Place dill pickle chips and sprinkle cayenne pepper if using and serve.

Nutrition: Calories: 281 Fat: 6 g Carb: 38 g Protein: 15 g

Chicken fried rice

Preparation time: 5 minutes

Cooking time: 20 minutes

Servings: 3

Ingredients:

- 1/2 cups cold rice
- 1/2 tbsps. Soy sauce
- 1 green onion, sliced
- 3/4 cup frozen vegetables of your choice
- 1/2 tsp vegetable oil
- 1/2 tsp sesame oil
- Salt as per taste
- 1/2 tbsp chili sauce (optional

Directions:

1. Add all of ingredients into a bowl and toss well.
2. Transfer into the air fryer baking accessory.
3. Place the baking accessory in the air fryer.
4. air fry in a preheated fryer at 340 °f for 12–15 minutes. Stir every 5 minutes.
5. Serve hot.

Nutrition: Calories: 420 Fat: 2 g Carb: 80 g Protein: 15 g

BEEF, STEAK AND LAMB RECIPES

Crumbed rack of lamb

Preparation time: 15 minutes

Cooking time: 30 minutes

Servings: 5

Ingredients:

- 1 tablespoon butter, melted
- 1 garlic clove, finely chopped
- 1 (1¾poundrack of lamb
- Salt and ground black pepper, as required
- 1 egg
- 1/2 cup panko breadcrumbs
- 1 tablespoon fresh thyme, minced
- 1 tablespoon fresh rosemary, minced

Directions:

1. In a bowl, mix the butter, garlic, salt, and black pepper.
2. Coat the rack of lamb with garlic mixture evenly.
3. In a shallow dish, beat the egg.

4. In another dish, mix the breadcrumbs and herbs.

5. Dip the rack of lamb in beaten egg and then, coat with breadcrumbs mixture.

6. Arrange the rack of lamb into the greased air fry basket.

7. Select "air fry" of air fryer oven and adjust the temperature to 212 ° f.

8. Adjust timer for 25 minutes and press "start/stop" to begin preheating.

9. When the unit beeps to show that it is preheated, insert the air fry basket in the oven.

10. Place the rack onto a cutting board for at least 10 minutes.

11. Cut the rack into individual chops and serve.

Nutrition: Calories: 696 Fat: 56g Carbs: 7g Protein: 22g

Sweet and Sour Delicious Pork

Preparation Time: 15 minutes

Cooking Time: 20 minutes

Servings: 4

Ingredients

- 1 pound 5 oz pork tenderloin, trimmed of fat, cut into strips
- 1 tablespoon corn flour (+ extra for coating)
- 4 oz red wine
- 10 oz tomato sauce or passata
- 1 tablespoon tomato paste or tomato puree
- 5 oz unsweetened apple juice
- 2 tablespoons brown sugar
- 2 sliced onions
- 2 cloves finely chopped garlic (optional)
- 2 tablespoons red wine vinegar
- 2 tablespoons olive oil
- Salt and freshly ground pepper to taste

Directions

1. Mix in a large bowl corn flour with red wine until smooth than add there: tomato sauce, apple juice, vinegar, sugar, tomato paste, season and mix thoroughly. Set bowl aside.
2. Coat chopped meat in corn flour and set aside.
3. Slice onions and put them into air fryer. Pour the olive oil over them. Cook for 5 minutes.

4. Add coated with flour pork and finely chopped garlic (optional). Cook for another 5 minutes.

5. Stir the pork to separate the pieces and add them to the sweet and sour sauce. Cook for 10 minutes or until the pork tender and the sauce thick.

6. Season to taste.

Nutrition: Calories: 291 Fat: 7g Carbs: 37g Protein: 22g

FISH AND SEAFOODS

Fried Crawfish

Preparation Time: 5 minutes

Cooking Time: 5 minutes

Servings: 4

Ingredients:

- 1pound crawfish
- 1 tablespoon avocado oil
- 1 teaspoon onion powder
- 1 tablespoon rosemary, chopped

Directions:

1. Preheat the air fryer to 340°F.
2. Place the crawfish in the air fryer basket and sprinkle with avocado oil and rosemary. Add the onion powder and stir the crawfish gently.
3. Cook the meal for 5 minutes.

Nutrition: Calories: 370 Fat: 21g Carbs: 27g Protein: 17g

Prawn Burgers

Preparation Time: 10 minutes

Cooking Time: 6 minutes

Servings: 2

Ingredients:

- ½ cup prawns, peeled, deveined and finely chopped
- ½ cup breadcrumbs
- 23 tablespoons onion, finely chopped
- 3 cups fresh baby greens
- ½ teaspoon ginger, minced
- ½ teaspoon garlic, minced
- ½ teaspoon red chili powder
- ½ teaspoon ground cumin
- ¼ teaspoon ground turmeric
- Salt and ground black pepper, as required

Directions:

1. Preheat the Air fryer to 390° F and grease an Air fryer basket.
2. Mix the prawns, breadcrumbs, onion, ginger, garlic, and spices in a bowl.
3. Make small sized patties from the mixture and transfer to the Air fryer basket.
4. Cook for about 6 minutes and dish out in a platter.
5. Serve immediately warm alongside the baby greens.

Nutrition: Calories: 184 Fat: 3g Carbs: 13g Protein: 26g

Jumbo Shrimp

Preparation Time: 5 minutes

Cooking Time: 10 Minutes

Servings: 4

Ingredients:

- 12 jumbo shrimps
- ½ tsp. garlic salt
- ¼ tsp. freshly cracked mixed peppercorns

For the Sauce:

- 1 tsp. Dijon mustard
- 4 tbsp. mayonnaise
- 1 tsp. lemon zest
- 1 tsp. chipotle powder
- ½ tsp. cumin powder

Directions:

1. Dust garlic salt over the shrimp and coat with the cracked peppercorns.
2. Fry the shrimp in the cooking basket at 395degreesF for 5 minutes.
3. Turn the shrimp over and allow to cook for a further 2 minutes.
4. In the meantime, mix together all ingredients for the sauce with a whisk.
5. Serve over the shrimp.

Nutrition: Calories: 148 Fat: 4g Carbs: 2g Protein: 24g

FRUIT AND
VEGETABLES

Mini zucchini's and feta

Preparation time: 10 minutes

Cooking time: 40 minutes

Serving: 4

Ingredients

- 12-ounce thawed puff pastry
- 4 large eggs
- ¼ cup milk
- 1 medium-sized thinly sliced zucchini
- 4 oz. Drained and crumbled feta cheese
- 2 tablespoon chopped fresh dill
- Olive oil spray
- Kosher salt as needed
- Freshly ground black pepper

Directions:

1. Preheat your fryer to 360 °f
2. Take a bowl and whisk eggs, season with salt and pepper
3. Add zucchini, feta, and dill to the mix
4. Stir well
5. Take 8 pieces of muffin tins and grease them up

6. Roll out the pastry and cut them into the bottom part of your tins (and the sides

7. Divide the egg mix amongst the tins and cook in batches (giving each batch about 15-20 minutes

8. Enjoy!

Nutrition Calories:201 Carbohydrate: 13g Protein: 11g Fat: 12g

SNACK RECIPES

Fried pickles

Preparation time: 15 minutes

Cooking time: 3 minutes

Servings: 6

Ingredients:

- 1 large egg
- ¾ cup almond milk
- pinch of cayenne
- 1 cup xanthium gum, divided
- ½ cup almond meal
- 2 tbsp fresh dill, chopped
- 2 tsp paprika
- 2 tsp black pepper
- 1 tsp salt
- 36 dill pickle slices, cold
- canola oil
- ranch dressing, for dipping

Directions:

1. Whisk together cayenne, milk, and egg.
2. Spread half cup xanthium gum in a shallow dish.
3. Mix the remaining ½ cup xanthium gum with almond meal, salt, pepper, dill, and paprika.
4. Dredge the pickle slices first through the xanthium gum then dip them in egg wash.
5. Coat them with almond meal mixture and shake off the excess.

6. Place them in the fryer basket and spray them with oil.

7. Return the basket to the fryer and air fry the pickles for 3 minutes at 370° f working in batches as to not crowd the basket.

8. Serve warm.

Nutrition: calories 138 total fat 12 g saturated fat 9 g cholesterol 31 mg mg total carbs 8 g fiber 8 g sugar 9 g protein 4 g

Crusted mozzarella sticks

Preparation time: 15 minutes

Cooking time: 5 minutes

Servings: 12

Ingredients:

- 12 mozzarella sticks string cheese, cut in half
- 2 large eggs, beaten
- ½ cup almond flour
- ½ cup parmesan cheese
- 1 tsp Italian seasoning
- ½ tsp garlic salt

Directions:

1. Mix almond flour with Italian seasoning, garlic salt, and parmesan cheese.
2. Whisk eggs in a separate bowl and keep them aside.
3. Dip the mozzarella sticks in eggs then coat with cheese mixture.
4. Spread them on a baking sheet lined with wax paper.
5. Freeze the sticks for 30 minutes then place them in the air fryer basket.
6. Return the basket to the fryer then air fry them for 5 minutes at 400°f.
7. Let them sit for 1 minute then transfer to a plate.
8. Serve.

Nutrition: calories 362 total fat 19 g saturated fat 9 g cholesterol 49 mg mg total carbs 1 g fiber 4 g sugar 1 g protein 23 g

Sesame nuggets

Preparation time: 15 minutes

Cooking time: 12 minutes

Servings: 6

Ingredients:

- 1 lb. chicken, cubed
- pinch sea salt
- 1 tsp sesame oil
- ¼ cup coconut flour
- ½ tsp ground ginger
- 4 egg whites
- 6 tbsp toasted sesame seeds
- cooking spray of choice

Directions:

1. Let your air fryer preheat to 400° f.
2. Meanwhile, toss the chicken cubes with sesame oil and salt.
3. Mix coconut flour with ground ginger in a Ziploc bag then place the chicken in it.
4. Zip the bag and shake well to coat the chicken well.
5. Whisk egg whites in a bowl then dip the coated chicken in egg whites.
6. Coat them with sesame seeds and shake off the excess.
7. Place the nuggets in the air fryer basket and return the basket to the fryer.

8. Air fry the nuggets for 6 minutes then flip them.

9. Spray the nuggets with cooking oil and cook for another 6 minutes.

10. Serve fresh.

Nutrition: calories 130 total fat 13 g saturated fat 4 g cholesterol 173 mg total carbs 9 g fiber 1 g sugar 2 g protein 77 g

Fried parmesan zucchini

Preparation time: 15 minutes

Cooking time: 16 minutes

Servings: 4

Ingredients:

- 2 medium zucchinis, sliced
- 1 large egg
- ½ cup grated parmesan cheese
- ¼ cup almond flour
- ½ tsp garlic powder
- 1 tsp Italian seasoning
- avocado oil spray

Directions:

1. Whisk egg in a shallow bowl and mix cheese, flour, Italian seasoning, and garlic powder in another.
2. Dip the zucchini slices in the egg then cheese mixture. Shake off the excess.
3. Place the slices in the air fryer basket and spray them with avocado oil.
4. Return the basket to the air fryer and air fry the slices for 8 minutes at 370° f.
5. Flip the zucchini slices and spray them with more oil.

6. Air fry them for 8 minutes more.

7. Cook them in batches.

8. Serve.

Nutrition: calories 139 total fat 6 g saturated fat 6 g cholesterol 67 mg total carbs 1 g fiber 3 g sugar 2 g protein 12 g

Radish chips

Preparation time: 15 minutes

Cooking time: 18 minutes

Servings: 6

Ingredients:

- 1 lb. bag of radish slices
- avocado oil or olive oil, enough to coat radishes
- salt, to taste
- pepper, to taste
- garlic powder, to taste
- onion powder, to taste

Directions:

1. Toss the washed radish slices with oil, salt, pepper, onion powder, and garlic powder.
2. Spread these slices in the air fryer basket and return the basket to the fryer.
3. Air fry them for 5 minutes at 370° f then toss them well.
4. Air fry the slices again for 5 more minutes.
5. Adjust seasoning with more spices and cooking oil.
6. Air fry these slices again for 5 minutes then toss them.
7. Cook for another 3 minutes.
8. Serve them.

Nutrition: calories 72 total fat 6 g saturated fat 4 g cholesterol 37 mg total carbs 6 g fiber 6 g sugar 6 g protein 8 g

APPETIZER RECIPES

Cremini mushroom satay

Preparation time: 10 minutes

Cooking time: 6 minutes

Servings: 2

Ingredients:

- 7 oz. Cremini mushrooms
- 2 tablespoon coconut milk
- 1 tablespoon butter
- 1 teaspoon chili flake
- ½ teaspoon balsamic vinegar
- ½ teaspoon curry powder
- ½ teaspoon white pepper

Directions:

1. Wash the mushrooms carefully.
2. Then sprinkle the mushrooms with the chili flakes, curry powder, and white pepper.
3. Preheat the air fryer to 400° f.
4. Toss the butter in the air fryer basket and melt it.
5. Put the mushrooms in the air fryer and cook it for 2 minutes
6. Shake the mushrooms well and sprinkle with the coconut milk and balsamic vinegar.
7. Cook the mushrooms for 4 minutes more at 400° f.
8. Then skewer the mushrooms on the wooden sticks and serve.
9. Enjoy!

Nutrition: calories 116 fat 5 fiber 3 carbs 6 protein 3

PASTA AND RICE

RECIPES

Lemony Parmesan Risotto with Peas

Preparation Time: 10 minutes

Cooking Time: 15 minutes

Servings 4

Ingredients:

- 1 tablespoon extra-virgin olive oil
- 2 tablespoons butter, divided
- 1 yellow onion, chopped
- 1½ cups Arborio rice
- 2 tablespoons lemon juice
- 3½ cups chicken stock, divided
- 1½ cups frozen peas, thawed
- 2 tablespoons parsley, finely chopped
- 2 tablespoons parmesan, finely grated
- 1 teaspoon grated lemon zest
- Salt and ground black pepper, to taste

Directions:

1. Press the Sauté button on your Instant Pot. Add and heat the oil and 1 tablespoon of butter.
2. Put onion and cook for 5 minutes, stirring occasionally. Mix in the rice and cook for an additional 3 minutes, stirring occasionally.
3. Stir in the lemon juice and 3 cups of stock.
4. Lock the lid. Select the Manual function and set the cooking time for 5 minutes at High Pressure.

5. Once cooking is complete, do a quick pressure release. Carefully open the lid.

6. Select the Sauté function again. Fold in the remaining ½ cup of stock and the peas and sauté for 2 minutes.

7. Add the remaining 1 tablespoon of butter, parsley, parmesan, lemon zest, salt, and pepper and stir well. Serve.

Nutrition: Calories: 317 Fat: 5g Carbs: 54g Protein: 11g

BREAD & GRAINS

Baguette bread

Preparation time: 15 minutes

cooking time: 20 minutes

Servings: 8

Ingredients:

- ¾ cup warm water
- ¾ teaspoon quick yeast
- ½ teaspoon demerara sugar
- 1 cup bread flour
- ½ cup whole-wheat flour
- ½ cup oat flour
- 1¼ teaspoons salt

Directions:

1. In a large bowl, place the water and sprinkle with yeast and sugar.
2. Set aside for 5 minutes or until foamy.
3. Add the bread flour and salt mix until a stiff dough form.
4. Put the dough onto a floured surface and with your hands, knead until smooth and elastic.
5. Now, shape the dough into a ball.
6. Place the dough into a slightly oiled bowl and turn to coat well.
7. With a plastic wrap, cover the bowl and place in a warm place for about 1 hour or until doubled in size.
8. With your hands, punch down the dough and form into a long slender loaf.

9. Place the loaf onto a lightly greased baking sheet and set aside in warm place, uncovered, for about 30 minutes.

10. Press "power button" of air fry oven and turn the dial to select the "air bake" mode.

11. Press the "time button" and again turn the dial to set the cooking time to 20 minutes.

12. Now push the "temp button" and rotate the dial to set the temperature at 450°f.

13. Press "start/pause" button to start.

14. When the unit beeps to show that it's preheated, open the lid.

15. Carefully, arrange the dough onto the "wire rack" and insert in the oven.

16. Carefully, invert the bread onto wire rack to cool completely before slicing.

17. Cut the bread into desired-sized slices and serve.

Nutrition: Calories: 114 Fat: 8 g Carbs: 28 g Fiber: 1 g Sugar: 3 g Protein: 8 g

DESSERT RECIPES

Red Wine Muffins

Preparation Time: 15 minutes

Cooking Time: 15 minutes

Servings: 6

Ingredients:

- 2 eggs
- 125g sugar
- Olive oil
- 50ml red wine
- A spoonful of hot water
- 75g cocoa powder
- 125g wheat flour
- 1 envelope of instant yeast

Directions:

1. Sift flour, cocoa, and yeast. In a bowl add eggs, sugar and mix with a blender until fluffy.
2. Incorporate oil, wine, and water while continuing to beat.
3. Add them dry and mix gently until homogenizing.
4. Place paper cups in a cupcake mold suitable for the Air Fryer.
5. Fill the mold up to ¾ of its capacity, take the Air Fryer programmed at 180°c for 10 - 15 minutes.
6. Allow to cool and Serve up with tea, coffee or milk.

Nutrition: Calories: 234 Fat: 11g Carbs: 31g Protein: 3g

Tea Cupcake

Preparation Time: 15 minutes

Cooking Time: 30 minutes

Servings: 6

Ingredients:

- 300g of water
- 2 teaspoons black tea
- 200g of nuts
- 4 eggs
- 300g sugar
- 250g sunflower oil.
- Vanilla
- 3 tablespoons of cocoa powder
- ½ teaspoon lemon juice
- 500g flour
- 1 envelope of instant yeast

Directions:

1. Prepare tea and Reserve up. Place the chopped nuts, the cold tea, eggs, sugar, and oil, vanilla, cocoa and lemon juice, mix 15 seconds at speed 5 in the processor.

2. Add flour and yeast, mix 20 seconds at speed 4.

3. Once you obtain a homogeneous mass, prepare a suitable mold, greased and bring Air Fryer for 20 to 25 minutes at 180°c.

4. Check the cooking and puncture with a stick, if necessary, put another 10 minutes, covered with a piece of aluminum foil

Nutrition: Calories: 160 Fat: 6g Carbs: 21g Protein: 2g

Rustic Cheesecake

Preparation Time: 15 minutes

Cooking Time: 35 minutes

Servings: 1

Ingredients:

- 100 g of unsalted butter.
- 75 g of sugar.
- 1 pinch of salt.
- 1 egg.
- 100 g of flour.
- 80 g of rye flour.
- 1 teaspoon instant yeast
- 250 g of cream cheese
- 1 egg.
- 40 g of sugar.
- 1 teaspoon vanilla sugar
- 1 pinch of salt.
- 200 g of currants

Directions:

1. Prepare a mold. Mix butter and sugar in a bowl; beat with a hand mixer until fluffy. Add egg, salt and beat.
2. Add the two flours, yeast and mix. There must be a manageable mass. Cover the bottom and walls of the mold with this mass.

3. Mix cream cheese, egg, sugar and salt, mix to eliminate lumps. Pour into the base that is in the mold. Place the currants to taste.

4. Bring the Air Fryer for 20 to 25 minutes at a temperature of 180° c.

5. Check the cooking, place aluminum foil and reprogram for 10 more minutes, or until golden brown.

Nutrition: Calories: 380 Fat: 28g Carbs: 50g Protein: 10g

Lemon Cake with Cheese Meringue

Preparation Time: 15 minutes

Cooking Time: 25 minutes

Servings: 4

Ingredients:

- Grated and juice of 1 lemon
- 3 eggs
- 1 cup of vegetable oil
- 2 cups flour
- 1 and ¾ cups of sugar
- 1 tablespoon baking powder
- 300g of cream cheese
- 1 can of condensed milk
- White chocolate.
- Vanilla essence to taste.
- 1 tablespoon of unflavored gelatin.
- 2 cups of milk cream.

Directions:

1. Place lemon, egg, oil, sugar, flour and baking powder in the blender. Process until a homogeneous paste is obtained.
2. Prepare the mold of the Air Fryer with wax paper and pour the mixture. Program it at 180°c for 20 to 25 minutes. Let stand, unmold and cool.
3. Meanwhile, dissolve the gelatin in water and set aside. Bring the chocolate cheese until melted.

111

4. Remove from the heat and add condensed milk next to the vanilla while stirring. Add the gelatin while mixing.

5. Apart whisk the cream to the point of snow and add to the previous mixture in an enveloping way.

6. Decorate the cake with the Preparation and refrigerate. Serve up cold with coffee or tea.

Nutrition: Calories: 430 Fat: 9g Carbs: 65g Protein: 9g

Creamy Sponge Cake

Preparation Time: 15 minutes

Cooking Time: 35 minutes

Servings: 1

Ingredients:

- 125g of cream cheese
- 30g of butter
- 70ml of milk
- 3 buds
- ½ teaspoon of salt
- Lemon juice
- 30g wheat flour
- 30g cornstarch
- 60g of sugar

Directions:

1. Prepare a mold. Place butter, cream cheese and milk in the processor. Add egg yolks and mix. Add salt and lemon juice.
2. Sift flour and cornstarch, keep mixing. Beat the whites until stiff, add the powdered sugar, little by little.
3. Join the two mixtures in three parts, with enveloping movements from top to bottom, until integrating.
4. Place in the mold and take the Air Fryer to a temperature of 160° c, for 20 - 25 minutes, check the cooking with a toothpick and cover with aluminum foil, cook for 10 minutes more if necessary.

Nutrition: Calories: 111 Fat: 5g Carbs: 14g Protein: 1g

Banana Inverted Cake

Preparation Time: 15 minutes

Cooking Time: 25 minutes

Servings: 1

Ingredients:

- 3 bananas cut horizontally
- 150g of butter
- ½ cup of brown sugar
- 1 cup of sugar
- Cinnamon
- Hot rum
- 2 eggs
- Vanilla
- 1 cup of milk
- 1 and ½ cup of flour
- 1 tablespoon baking powder
- 1 tablespoon of baking soda

Directions:

1. Place the bananas in the mold of the Air Fryer. Melt 50g butter in butter with ½ cup of sugar and cinnamon.
2. Then add the hot rum and light a fire with a match, when turning off remove from the heat and pour over the bananas.
3. Separate with a blender, mix butter and sugar until creamy. Add eggs, vanilla, and milk while stirring.
4. Sift flour, baking powder, baking soda and add it to the previous mix.

114

5. Beat in an enveloping way until it is integrated and poured over the bananas.

6. Program the Air Fryer at 180°c for 20 to 25 minutes, then cover with aluminum foil and program for 15 - 20 minutes.

7. Allow to cool and unmold by turning the mold. Serve up fresh.

Nutrition: Calories: 198 Fat: 9g Carbs: 28g Protein: 2g

<u>Yogurt Cake</u>

Preparation Time: 20 minutes

Cooking Time: 15 minutes

Servings: 1

Ingredients:

- 3 eggs
- 1 vanilla yogurt
- 2 cups sugar
- 3 cups rising flour
- 1 cup of oil
- Vanilla

Directions:

1. Beat the eggs with sugar until dissolved and add yogurt while stirring. Add oil little by little along with the vanilla.
2. Sift the flour and add it gently for 7 minutes.
3. Prepare the mold of the Air Fryer with waxed paper and pour the mixture. Schedule at 180°C for 15 - 20 minutes.
4. Cover with aluminum foil and program for 10 - 15 more minutes.
5. Let cool, unmold and serve.

Nutrition: Calories: 361 Fat: 11g Carbs: 59g Protein: 10g

CONCLUSION

Thank you for reading all this book!

Regardless of which diet you choose, keep in mind that the air fryer will significantly amplify the joy of the experience by allowing you to cook healthy meals that will seamlessly complement your lifestyle and your diet choice.

You have already taken a step towards your improvement.

Best wishes!

CPSIA information can be obtained
at www.ICGtesting.com
Printed in the USA
BVHW060035280221
601200BV00001B/79